THE LAUNDRY LIST
A guide to universal truths, issues and the possible road to serenity.

Kenneth Garett, Ph.D.

The Laundry List

Copyright © Kenneth Garett, Ph.D., 2012
All Rights Reserved

Williams Publishing Company
31822 Village Center Road, #102
Westlake Village, California 91361

Library of Congress Control Number: LCCN 2007935551
ISBN: 978-0-9666906-3-7

Cover Art by Liz DesRochers
All other art and design by Arte Moderno and Wild Beast Productions

Publisher's Cataloging-In-Publication Data
(Prepared by The Donohue Group, Inc.)

Garett, Kenneth.
 The laundry list : a guide to universal truths, issues and the possible road to serenity / Kenneth Garett.

 p. ; cm.

 ISBN: 978-0-9666906-3-7

 1. Peace of mind. 2. Happiness. 3. Self-acceptance. 4. Conduct of life. 5. Self-help techniques. I. Title.

BF637.P3 G27 2012
158.1   2012906052

Printed in The United States of America
10 9 8 7 6 5 4 3 2

Without limiting the rights under copyright reserved above, no part of this book may be reproduced, stored in or introduced into a retrieval system, or transmitted, in any form or by any means, without permission in writing from the publisher, with the exception for the inclusion of brief quotations in a review.

The Laundry List

This book is dedicated to the cherished memory of Marvin Meyers, Phd. An extraordinary man that I am honored to call my mentor and friend. His uncompromising candor and insightfulness walks with me daily..

The Laundry List

The Laundry List

ACKNOWLEDGMENTS

No journey is ever taken without helpers. I'd like to thank some of mine. These friends and relatives are a constant source of inspiration and we all need a good hit of inspiration on a daily basis.

To my children, Alexander and Renee: I can't possibly tell you how terrific it is to see both of you progress in your pursuit of higher education. I am particularly proud that both of you are entering the helping professions – choosing people's welfare over money as the core of your life work.

Laura Peck, who is now in her 80s, and who has transcribed all my books, including this one: Thanks for the years of support, constructive comments and hard work.

The Laundry List

The Laundry List

Contents

INTRODUCTION TO THE LAUNDRY LIST ... 9

IT'S UP TO YOU WHETHER YOU GET IT OR NOT THE INFORMATION IS ALREADY AVAILABLE ... 13

YOU ARE FREE TO THINK WHATEVER YOU WISH BUT DON'T TAKE YOUR THOUGHTS TOO SERIOUSLY ... 17

DON'T USE THE PAST AS AN EXCUSE ... 21

IT'S AMAZING HOW HAPPY PEOPLE ENJOY THE SMALLEST THINGS ... 25

LEARNING TO ENJOY YOUR OWN COMPANY IS A WISE THING TO PERFECT ... 29

ALL RELIGIONS DO IS TRY TO ANSWER QUESTIONS THAT CAN'T BE ANSWERED. WHAT'S WRONG WITH NOT KNOWING ANYWAY? ... 33

BEING PRESENT ISN'T AS EASY AS YOU THINK ... 37

THE OPINION OF OTHERS HAS LITTLE TO DO WITH WHO I AM ... 41

CONQUERING FEAR LEAVES A LOT OF ROOM FOR LIVING ... 45

LOVE IS NOT SUBTRACTIVE, YOU CAN ADD ON WITHOUT LOSING ANYONE ... 49

SILENCE IS A GOOD ALTERNATIVE TO SPEAKING UNKINDLY ... 51

LIVE FOR YOURSELF BUT NOT AT SOMEONE ELSE'S EXPENSE ... 55

EVERYONE TEACHES YOU SOMETHING – MOST PEOPLE TEACH YOU WHAT NOT TO DO ... 59

TO COMPARE YOURSELF TO OTHERS IS A QUICK TRIP TO NOWHERE ... 63

SO MUCH OF WHAT WE WERE TOLD GROWING UP NEEDS TO BE REMOVED SO WE CAN FIND OUR WAY ... 67

WEALTH HAS A WAY OF BECOMING LESS IMPORTANT WITH TIME ... 71

IT'S A RELIEF TO ACCEPT THAT NOTHING WILL EVER TOTALLY SATISFY YOU ... 75

THE PEOPLE YOU ENJOY MAKE UP FOR THE REST OF US ... 79

ALL SUFFERING COMES FROM NOT ACCEPTING "WHAT IS" ... 81

WHETHER YOUR LIFE MEANS ANYTHING IS COMPLETELY UP TO YOU ... 85

IF YOU REALLY WANTED IT, YOU WOULD ALREADY HAVE IT ... 89

LEARNING TO STOP JUDGING LEAVES LOTS OF ROOM TO LEARN ... 91

HAPPY PEOPLE HAVE ACQUIRED THE RIGHT WAY TO THINK, LIVE, AND FEEL ... 95

INTRODUCTION TO THE LAUNDRY LIST

Sometimes it takes a seed a long time to germinate. The seed that inspired the laundry list and the subsequent positive comments about the list from patients and readers has led me to be inspired to create a book about it. This seed was planted forty years ago by Sidney Kopp, Ph.D., an existential psychologist, whose book, *If You Meet the Buddha on the Road, Kill Him*, was given to me during one of my pilgrimages to Esalen Institute in Big Sur, California. This was a time in my life when I was a young psychologist in graduate school. The book's closing statement was a list called "The Laundry List", and I grew very fond of it. I still occasionally recommend it to readers.

The list was statements about "what is" - and my own list is further statements about "what is". This approach to "getting it" was intrinsically connected to the concept of a koan, a Zen statement, which demands one's focusing on some subtle issue of universal laws. That is precisely why Dr. Kopp's list, as well as a koan, never really lose their relevance when talking about universal truths and issues.

The intention of the koan is to shake oneself out of one's confusion into the present and to illuminate the clutter in our cerebral wiring. In so doing, this offers you the possible road to serenity.

Serenity seems to be very hard to come by for many of us. There seems to be some basic misunderstanding that humans seem to have which inhibits them from enjoying "what is". Eventually these misunderstandings lead to self-destructive behavior or dependence on religious doctrines that promise a state of grace but, in fact, offer a loss of independence of thought.

It is becoming increasingly more evident, with the passage of time, that I can only depend upon myself to figure out what a day means to me and what my life journey could be. I have completely abandoned the idea that anyone can really provide the core for you. That eliminates gurus, swamis, ministers, evangelical people, rabbis, and even psychological mentors. Undoubtedly they can be helpful in early stages of self-evaluation and for some a mentor is critical to prevent a fragile spirit from collapsing into despair.

Unfortunately many humans seem to have the predisposition to mental disorders which they have inherited and, with the stressors of daily life, they seem to need mentors in order to offer them guidance. In certain cases, this guidance needs to happen throughout their entire life. It is unfair to judge this dependency as much as it is unfair to criticize individuals with lifelong health problems.

The Laundry List

Ultimately, my truth-seeking now has become a personal journey. I have heard so many seekers, read so many religious texts, traveled to India, studied with many famous psychologists, only to come to the conclusion that I am completely responsible for figuring it out. I don't believe anyone really knew any more than I did in seeking the truth. This realization was quite liberating. Therefore, in certain ways, my journey ended.

Now I have the responsibility to realize what a day means to me and how to stay present. If I accomplish those missions, eventually my life will seem focused and purposeful.

The laundry list is a way of waking you up and helping you stay aware, like a committed meditator's daily practice. My hope is that it will make you smile and think and that will be sufficient for me.

The Laundry List

The Laundry List

IT'S UP TO YOU WHETHER YOU GET IT OR NOT THE INFORMATION IS ALREADY AVAILABLE

I distinctly remember, at 19, attending my first yoga retreat. It was held at a religious center north of Boston. The experience was quite transcendental. It inspired me to vegetarianism and complete sobriety from all mind-altering substances. The retreat was coordinated by Yogi Shri Khanna, an Indian man from Simla. He was a sturdily built individual with intense dark eyes and a strong physique honed by his many years of Hatha Yoga practice.

The memory of the building where the yoga classes were held has somewhat faded but I recall the Moody Blues "In Search of the Lost Chord" was playing and the otherworldliness of that moment had an enduring impact on me as a young university student.

Shri Khanna gave me a book that weekend called *How To Be A Yogi*", the traditional Indian depiction of the purity, commitment, and journey of a true yoga practitioner. I laugh hysterically when I see the bizarre transmutations of yoga sold in the U.S. today - be it Flow Yoga, Bikram Yoga, or Yoga Hip-Hop. I try not to be an arrogant purist as that smacks of religious orthodoxy, something which is all about judging and very short on wisdom.

One of the by-products of that weekend was the distinct impression on my part that there was some great universal truth hidden somewhere in the depths of this yoga experience, and that I had to find it one way or another.

I had never been inspired by my own religion to seek God through its tenets but somehow I was captivated by this magical idea of achieving a state of enlightenment or blissful detachment offered if I achieved it through my efforts.

In my own manner I pursued this ideal, studying another year with Yogi Khanna in Boston, then journeyed to India – visiting various yoga colleges and ashrams. The transformational power of these new revelations led me to psychology as it seemed the only profession whose basis was to unlock the hidden mysteries of the psyche. In some subtle way I retained the illusion that there was some secret that some of these yogis possessed and that being with them might permit a bit of that secret to rub off on me.

Fortunately, during this period of exploration, I ran across a simple book called *Zen Flesh, Zen Bones* authored by Paul Reps. It in some way redefined my view of what 'getting it straight' really meant. This redefinition was further assisted by attending Krishnamurti's lectures in Ojai, California. He insisted that he had no magical potion to clear up my confusion and ultimately I possessed the answer to my own life's puzzle and that, furthermore, there was no puzzle at all beyond the one I created.

This thinking led me to the hatching of what I fondly referred to as the egg that ended the search. The information is currently available at any moment. There is no journey and, in fact, the pilgrim mythology so prevalent in most religions is an internal process.

Let's proceed a little bit further with this type of thinking. There are no great men, only men; no great gurus, only yourself, and that the journey can end any moment you wish it to. The information is already available and always has been. No one can give it to you and, much like a butterfly, the experience that everything is in its perfect order, satori or inner bliss, will not last forever. The more you develop your inner appreciation the more these events will occur spontaneously but, much like everything else in the universe, the spiritual orgasmic moments will naturally ebb and return when they are appropriate.

There is no mystery at all. Religions have promised these absurd mystical precepts to capture members and keep them over the centuries. The answer is being present – closing off the rhetorical voices even if only momentarily and appreciating "what is". The only miracles are in nature and we had nothing to do with creating them in the first place but hopefully we can enjoy the majesty of nature's creation on a daily basis. That's probably the best joy – a subtle silent hike in a forest without any expectations and a moment of silence to appreciate its majesty.

YOU ARE FREE TO THINK WHATEVER YOU WISH BUT DON'T TAKE YOUR THOUGHTS TOO SERIOUSLY

I have a patient who suffers from Obsessive Compulsive Disorder commonly referred to in layman's terms as OCD.

When she was as young as 7, she began to be plagued by intrusive, negative thoughts. One prevalent thought pattern was that someone was going to break into her house as she laid in bed trembling late at night. She never shared most of these thoughts with her parents but many children do. Fortunately, some parents seek professional help so that the child no longer has to struggle with their inner demons alone.

By the time my patient was referred to me, her thoughts had become so immobilizing that she could barely drive a car; she feared leaving her parents as she was sure something horrific would happen to them in her absence.

Three years later, we have made great progress together, taming her voices. She is living away from home, attending university, and has even gone many months without seeking my help. There are moments when negative thoughts grip her and seem to propel her into a downward spiral of fear but, in general, she has tools to fight that and greater hopes she will have a normal life in spite of this condition. In her particular case, antidepressant medication has been a significant aid to control the biochemical imbalance that seems to be present in her entire family tree.

The relevance of this story is that, to some extent, we all struggle with our minds, our thoughts, and learning to cope with this stream of consciousness we possess is clearly a test for all of us, not just patients with Obsessive Compulsive Disorder.

The primary difference between most individuals and those with OCD is the relentless nature of the negative thoughts that OCD creates. I recall in the Hindu scriptures how the mind is referred to as a wild monkey and that, through meditation, the monkey can be subdued. Clearly, all of us have thoughts we don't share and that is totally fine – we are allowed that privacy – but thoughts can be powerful both in a positive and negative sense. Much of the more positive development in the past fifty years has been the recognition by psychologists and metaphysicians that directing your mind, programming your thoughts, can lead to happiness and success.

There are endless self-help programs now available based primarily on this principle – learning to enjoy the strange journey your mind takes and the way of finding peaceful living and not being attached to negative thoughts such as the possibility that bad things are going to happen

The Laundry List

Having the ability, deep in each of us of being capable of ultimate change to enjoy life is also a point. You can program that you are able to handle life's hiccups, as I refer to them, the endless continual challenges created by our complex modern world.

There are moments in the ticker-tape of thoughts that each of us constantly process, when our minds slow down and we are in the moment enjoying nature or engrossing activity. I certainly recommend we seek ways of experiencing these moments regularly. They seem to occur when we are calmer or involved in a pleasurable task, being involved in a deeper appreciations of being.

For example, I am currently in my cabin in the San Bernardino mountains. There is a warm breeze occasionally rustling the pine trees. Before me is the majesty of the mountains of this region. There is a bluejay squawking in a nearby tree. I feel truly blessed to have this moment. Everything seems in balance and I am busy writing, an activity that has become a friend. Writing is no longer a task as it was in university, writing as my daughter recently referred to it as my "personal legacy".

I can think anything I want be it loving, spiritual, violent, or sexual. I have no attachment to any of these thoughts. They will come and go and, if I wish, I can study them or just smile and let them pass. I don't need a guru or master to fix me, or adjustments I need to fix. My mind, and yours, can

The Laundry List

jump around. We can be amused by its gyrations or make a cardinal sin by taking it seriously.

That is your choice, and mine, at any moment – so think whatever you wish, just don't take your thoughts too seriously.

The Laundry List

DON'T USE THE PAST AS AN EXCUSE

Listening to people and trying to help them change their perspective on their own reality is not an easy job. There are moments when you realize how little you can do to help another person but, as I have shared with the future psychologists that I have trained over the years, if you do that very little well, you clearly have been successful in being a catalyst for psychic change.

We are all products of our childhood, both genetically and environmentally. We had no choice in what that phase of our life would be like. Who are parents were, how they treated us, was not something we chose. The era we grew up in, the people on our block, their values, religion, and their attitude toward us as children, were not our choice as well. Clearly, these events molded us in so many basic ways that ignoring the impact of our childhood experience would be grossly naïve.

Psychologists, beginning with Sigmund Freud, have developed various theories as to the impact these childhood experiences have in creating our adult lives. His process of therapy, outlined over 100 years ago, was to review these childhood events and attempt to work through the emotional obstacles created by them.

I have studied a number of techniques as well to accomplish this, including Gestalt, Reichian, bioenergetic, existential, cognitive, behavioral, Jungian, hypnotic, and neo-Freudian therapy techniques. All these approaches can be beneficial if applied by a skilled practitioner and a responsive client. There are also times when nothing works and we have to accept that some people are too damaged, either biochemically or developmentally, to benefit from treatment.

The older I get, the less likely I am to believe I have some magical alchemical treatment to cure everyone who enters my patient consultation room. Unfortunately many patients, and people in general, have learned to use their histories as an excuse. Inadvertently many psychologists, psychiatrists, and counselors have contributed to this process of self-deception by focusing too much time and energy rehashing the past and immersing themselves in the patient's endless need to explain and justify their misery. This is one of the primary reasons that traditional Freudian therapy has essentially faded from mainstream treatment. Beyond the fact the treatment was expensive and excessive in terms of time and the number of sessions, clinical research never showed it worked particularly well in changing the patient's actual life circumstances.

Behavioral approaches, which are goal-directed and more efficient, have become the primary path of much psychotherapy of this era. I don't want to imply that understanding your childhood or past experience is not important. It is valuable to piece together the basis of an adult's self-defeating behavior but there is a big difference between understand your problems and doing something to change them. Many patients understand why they are miserable but remain entrenched in their misery. I have frequently commented to them that I never get in the way of my patient's God-given right to be miserable. This paradoxical comment tends to force them to pay attention to themselves and stop looking at me as someone with a magic potion to cure them.

This is definitely a step toward taking responsibility for their current circumstances, something I highly approve of.

Let's return to this chapter's statement, don't use the past as an excuse. The implication that what has happened to you prevents you from acting and moving forward in a new direction is an ultimate falsehood. It is, in effect, saying that your current freedoms have been permanently diminished.

A woman I am presently treating was involved in a serious roll-over accident on the freeway. Passengers in her vehicle suffered significant injuries. Her fear of driving, when she came to me, was quite severe but the necessity to drive – since she lives in a rural area with no feasible mass transit – also was quite apparent. We decided to work toward slowly regaining her confidence and I would assist her in overcoming this basic fear. Conquering her fear was to be the integral part of what we would accomplish together.

The Laundry List

There are so many less obvious fears, however, that still restrict us - the fear of abandonment and intimacy, the fear of failure and fear of expressing one's independence or disappointing our parents. The list of inhibitors we face is endless but, from my perspective, they are excuses. Rather than accepting all these limitations, we can choose to overcome and conquer our current restrictions and obstacles. Your past is your history, your present is your reality. The freedom you currently possess is whether you wish to grow and challenge your fears or accept them as is. This is not an issue for me. I will accept you as you are. The question is can you accept yourself?

IT'S AMAZING HOW HAPPY PEOPLE ENJOY THE SMALLEST THINGS

I wrote this statement prior to a patient bringing in an article from the paper summarizing recent research done on the characteristics of people who have the gift of enjoying life.

Once again, as I explained in my previous book, *Happiness A Positive Addiction*, it is not wealth that is the best determinant of a person's level of happiness – but something much more subtle.

Yes, poverty, financial crisis, and want are predictive of unhappiness but, after a certain amount of money – enough to meet one's basic needs adequately, wealth and contentment just do not correlate. There are other factors which are much more relevant and the ability to enjoy the little things about the day say more about a person than the car you drive, your financial portfolio, or your wealth.

My regular comment to my patients is "I've never seen a person on his deathbed complain he didn't make enough money". It's not important at that point but most humans in their parting moments want to see the people who matter and experience their last moments on earth with them.

The Laundry List

Learning to enjoy the smallest things is, to some extent, a gift of nature. I recall my mother, years ago, sharing with me the feedback she received from the headmaster of the school, Crow Hill, I attended for my 4th grade. The summer before I started school there, the headmaster and his wife went on a journey across the United States, starting in Rhinebeck, New York and ending two months later back at the school.

For an amusing note, although my memories of the school are quite indistinct, I still recall the crows which were so prevalent on the hillside property and their endless cawing and noise.

The entire journey was done in a Volkswagen bus with the headmistress, Mrs. Crowley, her husband, and four students. I was by far the youngest of the group. We camped the entire summer and spent three weeks by a creek in Aspen, Colorado. It was a small, dusty town in the late '50s, not the posh center for the rich jetsetters it has become. We built a lean-to and fished with trout lines, catching the largest rainbow trout one could ever imagine.

Our itinerary involved traveling through numerous national parks, including Yellowstone, Rocky Mountain, and Glacier. We returned to the State of New York by the highway that crosses Southern Canada. The experience gave me my first real itch for travel – an itch I have been scratching for over 50 years, as well as a tremendous appreciation for the biodiversity that makes American such a wonderful visual experience.

The Laundry List

We visited Mesa Verde, Taos, The Garden of the Gods in Colorado, and many outstanding Indian archeological sites. The wildlife viewing was equally spectacular. A grizzly crawled over our sleeping bags at Glacier National Park. I still vividly remember hearing timber wolves howling through the night in Southern Alberta.

Without sharing the entire journey, I would like to return to the point which was Mrs. Crowley's comments to my mother. She told my mother "Kenneth showed more interest, asked more questions, and seemed more enthralled than the older boys throughout the journey". This was, for an 8-year-old boy, the best history book I ever read and my faded memories of the journey are still quite pleasant. I really enjoyed the little things we saw along the way – the birds, the flowers, the ever changing landscapes and, of course, the critters. I am still looking for them – be they the bobcats that amble through my property in the hills of Palm Springs or the deer that eat the daffodils in the early spring at my mountain cabin in Idyllwild, California.

To me, these events are not little things – they are the things that make life worth living. I particularly enjoy the sunrise in the early morning when I am driving to the swim center. There are so many small events that occur daily, I just try to appreciate as many of them as I can. Do you?

The Laundry List

The Laundry List

LEARNING TO ENJOY YOUR OWN COMPANY IS A WISE THING TO PERFECT

There is always a delicate balance that wisdom implies, a balance between work and play, between exercise and rest, and between alone time and socializing. This balance is idiographic, individual, and ever-changing.

In my earlier writings on personality, I described individuals as a combination of three basic tendencies, directing, isolating, and accommodating. Therefore, it is virtually impossible to determine how much time a healthy person needs to spend alone but inevitably we all have to learn how to be with ourselves. As we age, it appears spending time alone becomes increasingly more necessary.

Therefore, cultivating ways of enjoying being alone is worth addressing from the earliest days of our lives. To illustrate the point, most psychologists and early childhood specialists recommend, as early as 2 years of age, encouraging a child to sleep in their own bed – often in their own room – hoping the child acquires the ability to be alone in their room, playing with toys and eventually enjoying the pleasures of reading a good book by themselves. The balance between socializing and isolating is always a concern to sensitive parents who wish their children to be able to handle and enjoy others as well as themselves.

An interesting example of the diversity of the human need for privacy was clearly illustrated by a woman I knew for a brief period of time in my life. She was a neighbor of mine for some four years but I didn't encounter her until she had lived in my little community for over two years. She was in her late 30s, rented a small studio three doors down, had no pets and didn't date although she was quite attractive.

Our becoming friends was quite accidental. One day in mid-August the wash flooded, caused by a mountain rain storm. We were both forced to get out of our cars to enjoy the interesting natural phenomenon which seldom occurs in <u>August</u> although it is a frequent occurrence during the winter. The road was completely impassible due to a rush of water through the wash. The local TV station was there filming the event and interviewing local residents who were forced to turn around and use the alternative emergency road.

If we both hadn't been interviewed, I am fairly confident I never would have met her at all. It was a serendipitous encounter but her behavioral style helped me to understand isolators a great deal better than I had prior to our acquaintance. She didn't dislike people and had been unsuccessfully married some years before, but she had little need for us in her leisure hours. She spent the predominate amount of her time enjoying music, exercising, and reading – and did all these activities alone in her apartment. She eventually purchased a small house on a five acre property, down a dirt road, in a rural area of the Coachella Valley. She was a prototypic isolator but seldom seemed to have any qualms or regrets about her self-imposed isolation.

While I am not advocating her choices, she clearly had learned to enjoy her own company and was very protective of her privacy. For each of us, we have the challenge to learn to enjoy our alone time and seek time by ourselves as a refuge from the ever increasingly crowded world.

The statistics concerning the elderly indicate that there may well be a time when we live alone and have to create a reality of connecting to our own solitude.

In the course of my professional life, I have treated many desperate souls who have run from one love affair to the next, overlapping, for fear of being alone for even one night. This illustrates the danger of failing to develop the self-reliance of being alone and being content with being alone. It is wise to perfect the ability to enjoy being alone and seek moments of aloneness as a way of spiritually reconnecting to our inner world.

The Laundry List

ALL RELIGIONS DO IS TRY TO ANSWER QUESTIONS THAT CAN'T BE ANSWERED. WHAT'S WRONG WITH NOT KNOWING ANYWAY?

There seems to be an incessant universal craving, embedded in our DNA, for humans not to accept that certain things are unknown. This unexplained desire to solve problems – those which can be scientifically extricated from nature and those which seem beyond the grasp of empirical discovery have created a multitude of religions and theories all of which are ultimately difficult to prove.

Among these issues are such perplexing subjects as "who created the universe?", "is there some master intelligence impacting issues which affect our lives?", "does human existence extend beyond death in some alternative reality?"

The endless proliferation of religions has proposed numerous systems to explain these ultimately unresolvable questions; therefore very few of us were given the opportunity to develop our own conclusions concerning these matters. Our parents, with all the best intentions, shared with us their own religious affiliations and either kindly or forcibly made the vast majority of us attend religious classes – much of which were incredibly boring and tedious.

However, in the process of these Sunday School classes, our world view on these unanswerable questions was formulated. We were ultimately placed in a difficult quandary, either accepting the religious indoctrinations we received or rejecting them and seeking answers to these issues in some other manner. For most of us, it is far more expedient to just accept what we were told in spite of the gnawing doubt that exists because, at some level, most religious tenets are unprovable and ultimately, from an objective, scientific position, almost inconceivable.

Personally, I have vacillated between accepting the existence of post-death reality and, on the other hand, deciding that I really have no idea whatsoever and that, honestly, no one else does either.

The most frightening aspect of accepting any religion is that for many it implies the ultimate arrogance of deciding that your decision has guaranteed you a free pass after death to a good place and that all those who are non-believing will somehow be condemned to a less desirable outcome. This arrogance of belief has led to a human history of wars, crusades, jihads, and mass exterminations.

In a certain parallel consideration, the current warfare in the Middle East has remarkable similarities to the crusades of a thousand years ago with the major difference being our ultimate dependence on the oil provided by theses nations with emerging economies. Like with many cultures, the region's politics are intricately enmeshed within the expansion of the prevalent religious ideologies of those in, or seeking power.

The power of the groupthink prevalent in historical Christianity has led to massive forced conversions in the new world and Africa hundreds of years ago. Conversion as a goal still proliferates but without the violent enforcement prevalent in earlier years. This violence is now being imposed globally by Islam, or at least segments of Islam, which feel conversion and world domination is a justifiable vision.

The conclusion I have come to concerning religious matters is that I have no idea where we ultimately came from or where we are going – and no one else knows either. What is so wrong about accepting it all as a complete mystery?

The issue of overcoming our ultimate fear of dying becomes our only remaining substantive concern – an issue that needs to be approached and confronted whether one is religious or not. Clearly, it is easier and less frightening to believe that if we behave in accordance with some religious position, that we will be guaranteed a ticket to heaven, nirvana, or some universal paradise - even though our logical mind may see this as naïve and self-serving.

The Laundry List

My conclusion is simply – What's wrong with not knowing? Ultimately it is liberating and leads to a situation that I am espousing – which is to think for yourself on all matters whether political, moral, or religious and to accept that religions are man-made creations which over time become more dogmatic and frequently establish mental dictatorships over their members.

The Laundry List

BEING PRESENT ISN'T AS EASY AS YOU THINK

Being present seems that it would be an effortless undertaking. No matter what, we live in a constantly ever-changing now. I remember the enormous impact Baba Ram Dass' classic book had upon me in 1970. The book was entitled *Be Here Now..* Its stories and poems emphasized Richard Alpert's, aka Baba Ram Dass, search for serenity and mindfulness, results that led him to India and into intensive Yoga practice. The clutter and thoughts that consume all of us create unending amounts of background noise that makes living in the moment difficult and, for some, almost unattainable.

It is noteworthy that a healthy child, one without fear naturally, will be engrossed in the moment continuously, as will an animal that had not been abused, their consciousness shifts with the ever changing rhythm of the day.

Having sat with different humans for so many years, it is literally astounding how little time most of their consciousness was spent in the moment. Anxiety, probably the most prevalent psychological malady mental health professionals treat, is primarily based on futurizing negative possibilities or reviewing past catastrophic events.

The Laundry List

The reason so few people are able to stay focused in the present, is the continued difficulty they have with anxiety and how it impacts their awareness and consciousness of the moment.

In my last book, *Happiness A Positive Addiction*, I outlined a number of awareness exercises, including self-hypnotic techniques I utilize to help slow down the anxiety-ridden mind. All of them involve here and now awareness. These activities include breathing techniques, visual awareness exercises. The procedures are based on one basic principle: anxieties will spontaneously lift if a person's awareness shifts into the moment. My office is a safe haven, a time to face danger and a place to do it with assistance; the task before me is to motivate the anxiety-ridden patient to implement these procedures I teach at home and use them throughout the day to subdue the raging negative thoughts which prompted the pilgrimage to my office in the first place.

I was fortunate that these ideas, living from moment to moment, were offered to me quite early in my life. I saw the possibility of enjoying the moment and seizing the present as a crucial element of being in a joyful reality.

Inevitably, our brains are hardwired with memories and unending assumptions which make us travel between the present, past, or future, an endless ongoing process. Listening, smiling, and accepting the inevitability of the back-and-forth between the world and the stream of consciousness allows calmness and acceptance to occur. Moments of silence, both in meditation, or just breathing or looking and receiving are always available to re-engage you with the now. I used to think that somehow my early years of Yoga study would achieve a continual state of awareness of now. It is described as "samadhi" in the Yoga scriptures.

In India, I encountered masters deemed, at least to an outside observer, to be in a state of higher consciousness all the time. One man in Lonavla, at the Yoga College, seemed to spend his entire day lying in a trance state in a bed surrounded by mosquito netting. On occasion, he would arise and have a lassi, a yogurt drink, walk around, and then return to his bed. He was revered as an enlightened soul. He never spoke at all but lived in his ever continuous own reality.

I also described another wise man in my book, *You Are Already Perfect*, who was in the world, living alone, doing jumping jacks and feeding stray dogs. He was extremely kind to me, a lost soul, who knocked on his door during my journey to Rishikesh, one of the centers for ashrams in Northern India.

While possibly these individuals did achieve their every minute Zen, or Samadhi, while in the living state, but it has not happened to me – at least not continuously, so I stopped seeking it. The seeking of a State of Good or Contentment is like chasing your own shadow - better do the work of staying present and if it is meant to happen, so be it. In the meantime, I'm content to focus on enjoying every moment and taking in the experience of my brief human time without looking forward or looking backward.

THE OPINION OF OTHERS HAS LITTLE TO DO WITH WHO I AM

Fortune comes in many ways. One, of my more fortunate experiences as a young man was finding *Zen Flesh, Zen Bones* in a bookstore at the University of the Americas in Cholula, Mexico. It contained Zen stories that I utilized as a guidepost in my book, *You Are Already Perfect*. The essence of one of these stories led me to write a chapter in that book entitled "What Other People Think". Essentially it is a chapter that explains the old Zen story "Is That So?"

It is a story of an old monk who refuses to defend himself when he is accused of impregnating a neighbor's daughter. The situation of being falsely accused, and his reaction of no reaction, gave me clues as to how to keep my life together.

One, live for yourself. without expecting approval or commendation, including not overreacting to criticism.

Secondly, what people think has little to do with your deeper self.. What they perceive of you hardly matters. This clearly doesn't mean we should completely ignore feedback we receive from others – especially feedback from multiple sources.

The Laundry List

Learning how we affect others is important but not critical. Life isn't a popularity contest. It is amazing how other's perception of someone changes once they become aware of a person's true world and private life – not the ideal life created by one's transcript of living. Tiger Woods' recent debacle, President Clinton's impeachment, and O.J. Simpson's exposure and trial are all examples of how popularity can plummet once the human inner demons are revealed.

With the majority of us however fame, or the thoughts of fame are not important. We struggle and seek external positive feedback from loved ones and friends. These are more crucial issues in our emotional development.

Unfortunately, it's an unending cycle, the more you need approval for who you are or what you do, brings you into the quagmire of insecurity.

This process begins long before we have a clue as to the insidious nature of its consequences. The need for positive feedback from our parents extends to our teachers, peers, and ultimately everyone who knows us. We become dependent on this feedback and external approval is an easy trap to come to, but ultimately looking to others for support and inspiration is a dangerous and disheartening process.

Inevitably, we all have to choose our life's journey and if we allow others to dictate the terms of our journey, one day we will realize that we have cheated ourselves of the opportunity of experiencing our unique talents. In therapy, so many patients come suffering from anxiety, fear of choosing the wrong person, occupation, or direction. They look to me to solve this issue. They seek my approval and in so doing, re-create the negative behavior that got them confused in the first place. Ultimately, I respect the inner wisdom of my patients themselves, and in most cases I believe if given the opportunity to regain their self-esteem, they will make better choices based on their own unique perception of who and what they are meant to be. Therapy isn't telling people who to be but giving them the time and permission to find that out for themselves.

Ultimately, the independence of action does not create a world of selfish, greedy egotists. That is the end product of people's view that money, power and control can create some focus to their lives. Real independence involves respecting the right of others' independence as well as creating an attitude of self-acceptance which extends into acceptance of others.

Learning that ultimately, no matter what you choose, someone will want you to do otherwise is liberating as it refocuses you on your own life's direction. Re-read Thoreau's *Walden Pond* and his marvelous journey in his self-study, or Ayn Rand, in *The Virtue of Selfishness* - another friend of my adolescent days which made me rethink contemporary religion as well as altruism. Focusing on living for yourself and realizing that no one really knows how you experience the world around you, can help you accept that others will always have their opinions and you need give little weight to their opinions as to who you ultimately choose to be.

The Laundry List

CONQUERING FEAR LEAVES A LOT OF ROOM FOR LIVING

If there is a theme in my written work, it is clearly that we are all prisoners, to some extent, of some form of self-limitation. Much of our self-imposed restrictions were created by the endless admonitions we heard growing up.

I still vividly recall one of my childhood fears. It was a fear of entering a church which was located at the end of our block at Marborough Road in Brooklyn. Somehow I had heard that churches were forbidden places to Jews and that horrible things could happen if you entered one. There was a large oak tree located near the church where I would collect acorns in the fall. I looked at that building, while stooping to pick them up, with a mixture of respect and trepidation which remained until we moved to another neighborhood when I was 10 years of age. Slowly, the church drifted into my memory.

For a touch of humor, I drove down that block a few years ago during one my regular pilgrimages to Brooklyn, only to be surprised that the once formidable building had been converted, some years ago, into a synagogue. I wonder if they tried to exorcise all the Christian spirits in the building as part of the conversion process.

The Laundry List

It took many years to completely overcome my feelings of discomfort entering a church. I do feel, however, that the fear proved an important experience by instructing me as to how easy it is to develop phobic or irrational fears of places and things.

Once I overcame this sense of dread I began to enjoy the immense architectural and cultural history of the old churches of Cholula, Mexico, a town with a reputation for having a church for every day of the year. That claim, however, is somewhat exaggerated but, for a small provincial town of Central Mexico, the municipality there has over 200 churches. Many of these churches are still functioning with regular services and Masses.

The essential point I'm making is, if I hadn't overcome my childhood anxiety concerning churches, I never would have enjoyed the Sistine Chapel or the great cathedrals of Segovia and Madrid. Fear has far more reaching ramifications than merely limiting a small boy from entering a church. The self-restricting components of fear continue to invade my office with endless permutations as new patients arrive.

It continues to be a challenge of mine to help others push past their impasses and fears. To be a sincere advocate of fear dissolution, I have begun to work with myself. Lately, intermittently, I practice an exercise imagining, during a meditation, that my energy has left my body and I am dead. This may seem like a bizarre or maudlin activity but it has made me much more accepting that dying can be a painless journey to wherever.

I intend to continue this exercise for the rest of my life. It isn't a unique practice. The Tantric Buddhists and the Tibetan Buddhists describe such meditative activities in the Tibetan *Book of the Dead*. Once fear is conquered, the necessity to live fully can be totally embraced.

Humans have so many fears - fear of failure, fear of being alone, fear of public humiliation and ridicule. The list of phobias is seemingly endless and ever-growing,

I recently discharged a patient who came to me with an extreme fear of cockroaches. The fear had become so pervasive that she had to sleep in a tent in her own living room. Living in the constant fear of being emotionally overwhelmed by a roach in her house, she was physically drained and tearful in many of our early sessions. Fortunately, through the utilization of cognitive treatment and some internal metamorphic or transformational process, she eventually calmed down and seemed to be more in control of her life. When compared to other individuals, she still reacts negatively to roaches but her body language is more relaxed and they no longer possess and torment her as they once did.

Another great fear that most of us ignore, but clearly is extremely self-limiting, is the fear of trying new things, exploring new activities, or expanding new relationships.

The Laundry List

Humans are ritualized creatures and these life patterns can prevent allowing us to fully experience the variety of life's possibilities. Life's end is not tragic but not living fully is, so give yourself room to have a full life, identify and overcome your self-imposed restrictions. You will be amazed by how much room for living you will have.

LOVE IS NOT SUBTRACTIVE, YOU CAN ADD ON WITHOUT LOSING ANYONE

Becoming a compassionate, loving soul is a great challenge. There is such fear of being hurt, being rejected, or being misunderstood when we love. The greater a persona's ability is to see the good around him, the more capable he or she is to be caring.

Love is such a confusing word. Interestingly enough, it is defined in the dictionary as "a strong affection or liking for someone or something". Alternative definitions involve passionate affection but the first definition given implies liking – a positive transfer of energy toward another.

The better we feel about ourselves, the more accepting we are of our unique essence, the more it seems we can like others. The more open we become, the less judgmental, the more we can accept the differences that we note in the world around us. The more tolerant I can be toward the diversity in our culture, the more I receive that tolerance back. It's just the law of attraction in the affective domain.

The view of love that I am discussing has nothing to do with the possessive love of a jealous lover or controlling parent. This view of love I am espousing stems from the opinion that an open soul will meet many people they can embrace and care for.

People are not meant to be possessed by love but by the loving ideal. This has been distorted by popular writers from time immemorial. If passionate love leads to heartbreak, violence, and sadness, I question whether it is love at all.

I think the best analogy about my view of love is that of a parent having their second child. The great love most healthy parents experience with the birth of their oldest isn't reduced by the birth of their second child. We can accommodate both children and add more caring to ourselves and our lives. In so doing, we become a deeper pool of caring.

SILENCE IS A GOOD ALTERNATIVE TO SPEAKING UNKINDLY

Insulting someone is worse than cheating him financially. Money can be returned but pain caused by words cannot be erased. (Choshen Mishpat 228:1) This old Judaic statement of wisdom indicates the severity considered by unkind words. The term "Loshon Hora", negative gossip, and its opposite, which is guarding your tongue, is far more challenging than overt acts of violence. There are admonitions against gossip in Talmudic Law. There are so many that they exceed the number of admonitions against murder. They consider gossip as killing someone while they are still alive.

The challenge of turning away from negative words and slanders is far more difficult than one can ever imagine. We, and when I say we, I absolutely include myself, all have undisciplined programs which were developed early in our childhood of speaking our mind, either in a positive or negative way, whenever we choose to.

This lack of verbal restraint has two essential outcomes. One, is hurting people's feelings inadvertently. Another, probably a far more profound effect, is embedding all of us in a critical, negative mind set, which in many ways inhibits the development of a quiet mind.

The Laundry List

Some of my readers probably need a more detailed explanation of what is meant by the "Zen Mind" and I am willing to share a basic tenet to illustrate the principle of non-judging.

There is a short story in the book, *Zen Flesh, Zen Bones* about a Zen student who went to a butcher and requested the butcher's best meat; at which point the butcher replied, "all my meat is the best". This response enlightened the student and made him aware there is no way to determine what is best – meaning delineations of good, bad, best, not best, fat, thin, smart, stupid, divide the world into arbitrary categories that continue to stimulate our judging, critical intellect.

The admission of this mind-set forces us into the world of "being" not "judging". Unkind words are usually the end product of judging, a lack of compassion, and our childhood mind-set which was taught to us through our parents.

Personally, I feel I have made very little progress in this area in spite of all my training. I am keenly aware of doing it and regularly laugh at myself at the absurd notions that my judgments are, in fact, a meaningful way of responding to the world around me.

An exercise in "being" that seems to help is a long walk in a forest where one can observe, enjoy the trees, birds, squirrels, or whatever appears, without comment or judgment. Just observe the world, breathe, and participate. Then you can become more aware of the harsh judgments that pass through your mind and the inner voices which lead us to speak in an unkind manner.

If you don't want this negative mind-set and its voices to operate freely and definitely, well, start by observing it. Don't judge it as a part of you. See if you can make a truce with your inner critic. Then speaking unkindly will occur less often and when you speak unkindly you will realize that silence is always a viable alternative.

The Laundry List

The Laundry List

LIVE FOR YOURSELF BUT NOT AT SOMEONE ELSE'S EXPENSE

When I created this statement, it was a spontaneous modification of my much revisited adolescent reading of Ayn Rand's *The Virtue of Selfishness*. This book was introduced to me in health class by my teacher at Midwood High School at age 14, a book whose controversy led to him being removed from the school one year later.

The book confronts the conceptualization that neither altruism nor do-goodism are necessary or worthy aspirations. So much of Judeo-Christian ideology is based on the principle of charity and helping others, placing these acts as the ultimate responsibility of any decent human being.

Tzedakah, giving charity, is considered the moral obligation of any responsible Jew; God approves of such acts, it is declared in the ancient scriptures. Since I haven't spoken to God recently, I can't confirm that He actually holds charity in such high regard but, historically, self-sacrifice and even martyrdom were considered the highest acts of human virtue.

But are these principles ever really analyzed critically? The underlying principle of getting to heaven because one was charitable is probably as absurd as the idea that heaven actually exists at all.

Let's discuss the idea of living for yourself. To me, this concept means that the life you choose is your own, not based on your parents' roadmap. Your actions are based on what pleases you without apology or compromise. You essentially live by your own inner spirit, or anima, and the force you exert into life can be directed by what you declare as relevant for yourself.

However there is a hitch, a glitch in this philosophy of self-centeredness that this journey to individualism needs to address. Using others, hurting others indiscriminately, in the process of one's self-pursuit is in effect a contamination or violation of the principle of individualism, or at least the elevated form of individualism that I am discussing.

Let's redirect this to discuss family life. When we choose to become parents, a rather immense undertaking to say the least, that choice to parent indicates you are willing to temper that selfishness so as not to injure the child you have chosen to create.

The enormity of that responsibility becomes all the more apparent in the case of divorce. Unfortunately, human beings don't get along that well. Marriage is by far the most demanding human relationship that exists and frequently fails. The combining of sexual needs, financial responsibility, communication patterns, and family issues including child-rearing problems into a positive, workable team is something few couples ever achieve. The inability to sustain all these factors is the basis of family breakups and divorces will always occur due to the complex nature of the human psyche.

The relevance to this issue is that parents have to choose how much the children will suffer due to the division of their household. That is where tempering living for yourself is necessary if you wish to have a sense of contentment when your children are grown. Many parents seek freedom at the expense of their children. Many families suffer because this delicate balance is not considered by one or both of the parents during the separation process.

So seek the life you wish but if you choose family life, consider the sacrifice of your eccentricities as part of the equation. Children are optional in today's world. Many couples opt to be childless and that is a respectful choice as the journey to parenthood is a demanding one with many rewards but a plethora of obligations.

The Laundry List

The Laundry List

EVERYONE TEACHES YOU SOMETHING – MOST PEOPLE TEACH YOU WHAT NOT TO DO

This brief statement was shared with me as a young man by my Yoga teacher, Shri Khanna, in Boston at a retreat. His comment was made in context of the government and the then overwhelming tension created by the war in Vietnam. He was trying to help his students see that more violence and anger in response to our frustration after the Kent State shooting was of no value, that in fact we had to develop a more refined, loving attitude toward the madness of that era or become part of the insanity ourselves. He gave me a book by Mahatma Gandhi on soul power and I saw that becoming a violent, antiwar militant would be turning into the very thing that I detested in the first place.

Unfortunately, reverse learning is probably the most common way to see what to avoid. I have always used people who have destroyed their lives as examples of ways of learning. The best example of that is found in a chapter of a book I wrote some years ago, *You Are Already Perfect*, when I described the life of my ex-roommate, Arthur Ducore. The chapter was titled, "Life is a Six-Pack of Beer". The story was the life of Arthur Ducore, my freshman roommate at Boston University, who died of alcoholism at age 40. If you haven't read the chapter, please do. It is the sad tale of a young man with certain personality vulnerabilities who, with the help of drugs and alcohol, ended his life all too soon.

So many people around you can teach you in a backward manner. You observe their behavior and try to avoid their mistakes. This isn't as easy as it sounds especially when it comes to your parents. So much of your parents' behavior, whether you wish to admit it or not, was internalized during your early childhood that, honestly speaking, in certain ways they continue to live within you in terms of your personality.

Psychologists refer to these sub-personalities as "interjects". These interjects, if not understood, can literally create havoc in your personal life. So, in all honesty, most of us can learn what not to do by being a discerning observer of our own self.

Admittedly, in spite of a lifetime study of psychology and a poignant understanding of my own demons, I have come to see that occasionally they will act up anyway.

I have come to the conclusion that these demons are life-long companions and it is better to know them so at least you are not working in the dark. What I mean by this is that at least you don't have to ask why you do what you do. Why you do certain things is clearly understood once you comprehend the nature of your interjects.

The Laundry List

Much of the AA 12-Step Program involves the process of knowing these demons and interjects. This is the extensive work of the Step 4, which is a personal inventory. In a sincere inventory, one begins to understand the internal conflicts which led to their dependency on drugs and alcohol in the first place.

As life passes, our issues change and this inventory needs updating and revision throughout the course of a lifetime.

So learn from the folly of others but take the plunge and learn from your own inner voices. If this idea seems too abstract, start by writing down some of the ways you deal with key figures in your life: your life partner, your supervisor, co-workers, and relatives. See if any pattern emerges.

Good luck in figuring out the complex and unique puzzle that you are!

The Laundry List

The Laundry List

TO COMPARE YOURSELF TO OTHERS IS A QUICK TRIP TO NOWHERE

It all begins so innocently, at home, in preschool, your parents – your behaviors and attitudes are compared to siblings, peers, and to some standard set by your parents and teachers. They create a standard you feel you should meet and the standard continues to change throughout your formative years. Grades appear and your class rank and your SAT scores, the university you get admitted to.

The process of being compared continues on the playground, in team sports. Everywhere you look it becomes second nature to determine your success or failure in terms of others.

Then the mating ritual begins with the successful and the less successful; the prom queens and the football stars; the winners and the also-rans. Interestingly enough, even the so-called winners in the comparison game seem tainted by self-doubt even though they appear to have everything going for them.

This game of external determination of value continues into adulthood. The car you drive; how much money you make; your status in the community – endless external ways of feeling **OK**. But ultimately somehow it all pulls us further and further and deeper and deeper into comparing ourselves to others.

The outcomes of this adventure are feelings of inferiority or a continuous striving to not lose the false sense of wellbeing creating by our status seeking.

How do we free ourselves from this? After so many years of trying to reach the top of the pyramid it is hard to accept the journey doesn't produce the desired results. Even more difficult is to start to appreciate yourself without an external standard of comparison. The inevitable consequence of comparing yourself is that the uniqueness of you is never fully appreciated.

The process of stopping your mind from the endless cycle of comparisons, and the discontent implicit in this process, begins with fully embracing how deeply embedded we all are in it. Americans' idolization of super models, movie stars, rock stars, and athletes make small children develop a hero-worshiping mentality and the implied concept that somehow being yourself isn't quite good enough. How to develop a standard for who you want to be based only on yourself, without external guidelines or any other comparisons, isn't easy.

The Laundry List

Fortunately, this is all addressed in Buddhism and Taoism. There is an old Buddhist story of how a student of Zen became enlightened after a butcher replied to his question of which of his meat was the best. The butcher answered by saying that all of his meat was the best, leaving the student to understand there is no way to judge the best. Therefore, ultimately there is no way of judging yourself.

The realization of getting past judging and comparing yourself to others is a goal in attitude based on self-reliance from an emotional standpoint. It is ultimately another one of those unattainable quests that can be accomplished in one moment if we allow it. The contradiction is realizing that you are valuable without comparison creates the security effortlessly. It then becomes a lifetime of reminding yourself endlessly when you fall back into the cycle of comparison again.

Being better or worse is a state of dualism, creating ways of defining your value. Who can say what anyone's value is anyway?

The Laundry List

SO MUCH OF WHAT WE WERE TOLD GROWING UP NEEDS TO BE REMOVED SO WE CAN FIND OUR WAY

"Men and books lie....only nature never lies." Thomas Paine.

It is truly remarkable how much distorted information we are fed growing up. It takes a lifetime to eliminate the oceans of superstition and to start learning to think for yourself.

Clearly, there are a few culprits that I believe are busy promoting the propaganda I am concerned about. One, clearly, is organized religion which William James referred to as "a monumental chapter in the history of human egotism."

The second is a very self-serving view of American society and American values that we were fed throughout our educational process. Even worse is combining these two forces of religion and government in religious schools.

It was truly shocking to read a revisionist historian such as Howard Zinn, one of my professors at Boston University, whose history of the United States presents a very different picture of America than I learned in public school. His writing shows the extreme distortion presented by traditional history book writers who present the American expansion as some divine, spiritual act of goodness and the spread of democracy and Christianity as a moral mission.

Fortunately, I came of age during the Vietnam conflict, a time when many young Americans were questioning the veracity and decency of our government's participation in international policing and meddling. Unfortunately, in reviewing recent world events, it appears little was learned from our failures of that era.

Another, probably more critical, area of things that need to be removed is the self-imposed limits that we were told about ourselves growing up. So few parents truly allow their children the gift of exploring their own possibilities without interference. It takes a highly enlightened individual to trust the essential wisdom of a child to choose the proper path for himself. We parents harbor, either consciously or unconsciously, all sorts of prejudices and plans about what our children should be. A joke I frequently share illustrates this point – my mother said I was free to be any type of doctor I chose.

Realizing the gift of not imposing your value system on a child is one rarely achieved. The information shared usually has to do with religious values, prejudices, and attitudes about what is important, or not.

The Laundry List

Whether you help a child develop a sense of trust in his own wisdom or burden him with guilt and self-doubt, based on your own criticism and comparison, is another significant and powerful issue to consider in terms of your parenting approach.

Finally, developing your own sense of values and seeking your own truth at times means releasing the program we were given as children. It is being brave enough to discard what you were told as truth so that you can discover that for yourself.

The Laundry List

WEALTH HAS A WAY OF BECOMING LESS IMPORTANT WITH TIME

The passing of time makes us realize that our visit here is a very short journey. I have never heard of someone on his or her deathbed regretting that he or she had not made more money in their life. At that point, the only thing that truly matters is the fading connection with the people they cared for during their time on this planet. The end clarifies what is important, or not, to many who have spent their lives consumed by money accumulation. It is better to figure that out before the time has passed than to mislead oneself about the truly important issues facing us on our life's sojourn.

I have continually affirmed that money is only partially related to life contentment. There is a relationship between money and happiness in that poverty and want create emotional suffering, but once a person has sufficient financial means, a home, a car, all the electrical gadgetry that the 21th century promotes as necessary, how do we explain the discontent we see around us in spite of all these possessions?

Learning to enjoy the passing of a day has little to do with money. In reviewing the things I enjoy most, they have little to do with my assets and possessions – many of them cost nothing at all such as walking in the mountains, listening to the sounds of the morning, enjoying a friend or the subtle changes as twilight approaches. These are far more enduring than any material possessions.

Another phenomenon that has impacted my impression of the issue of the importance of defining one's values about money, are the endless people who share with me their discontent about their jobs or vocation. There are always money concerns or fear of change that lead someone to spend many years of their life working at a job they dislike. I particularly notice that public servants diligently count the years until they can retire with their pensions. Unfortunately the time they spend in unhappy work is not refundable and I have become increasingly more aware that job status is an important factor in one's general dissatisfaction about other aspects of their life.

The older we get, the more apparent it is that time will not be recaptured and the pursuit of money and the illusion of security it implies is an exercise in futility. Either you enjoy the day or you don't. It's really that simple. Whether your assets increase or decrease that day will mean very little when your days are few.

The issue to this writer seems to be whether you will feel you had a full life, one which encompassed a meaningful experience for you, with no regrets, no should haves, no "I missed the boat".

The Laundry List

What impact did your life have on others on the planet is also an important issue. Can you enjoy a simple day without concern? Are you able to extricate yourself from the meaningless materialism promoted by our culture and its most recent creation, reality TV - a bizarre fascination with people, mostly wealthy, whose behavior is remarkably unremarkable?

So plan for your future, but retain the wisdom to realize that money, and its acquisition, will not create meaning, purpose, or contentment. These are the end-products of finding your unique way of being on the planet for the limited time we are afforded.

The Laundry List

The Laundry List

IT'S A RELIEF TO ACCEPT THAT NOTHING WILL EVER TOTALLY SATISFY YOU

There is a strange phenomenon that occurs after a person completes a Ph.D. I don't know if there are any research articles documenting it, but it has been noted by many of my friends. There is a certain emptiness and lack fullness that happens once they graduate. The journey to the degree took so much effort that, once done, there is a sense of "is that all there is"? – so I created the term, the Ph..D. Blues, to describe it.

This phenomenon happens in many other aspects of life. The more we seek, it seems the more we need to seek. A few examples are the endless accumulation of possessions and money. When is enough enough? Must we endlessly seek the constant excitement of a new lover, a new experience or a new possession?

The cycles of wanting seem endless and this constant seeking is an essential theme of Buddhist thought. Somehow, accepting that no matter what you get there will always be a little voice that craves more, is a great relief. It will awaken the reality that seeking and wanting leads to more of the same.

You may respond, why try to accomplish anything if ultimately it won't totally satisfy you? Well, try anyway and strive, but just remember there is no way to totally satisfy that part of yourself. There will always be another goal, another place to go and another desire to fulfill. That's just the way the ego is, it always wants more.

The relief that realizing that we can never totally satisfy ourselves brings is quite refreshing. Instead of expecting the arrival of someplace of total contentment, we can embrace its impossibility and laugh at the entire issue. What this implies is that one achieves the ability to not take oneself so seriously. The illusion that getting what you want is important can be revisited from a completely different perspective; that the reality is what you want may be very unimportant in terms of the universe or, once you acquire it, that your life will change in any profound manner whatsoever.

The thought process that leads to this self-deception is worth revisiting for a minute. For example, I will be happy when I retire, or when I'm married with children, or when I acquire a certain possession, relate to the same constant striving of the ego's needing more for some sense of fulfillment.

Unfortunately, there is ultimately nothing you can do to be happy or to have enough. This places the end-product of an internal evolution that has little to do with striving but a lot to do with appreciating. To appreciate the gift of being and to be at peace now takes stopping all the assumptions that have been fed to you throughout your entire life and learning to watch your mind, at least momentarily, and appreciate what is at this very moment.

The realization that nothing will ever totally satisfy you can be very satisfying in itself. It makes one reconsider the constant seeking and striving and offers the possibility of appreciating what you already have.

The Laundry List

The Laundry List

THE PEOPLE YOU ENJOY MAKE UP FOR THE REST OF US

In life we meet an endless number of fellow humans. They come in and out of our existence having various levels of impact upon us. A rare few of them have what I consider to be an enduring impact upon our lives. These people are worth the incredible aggravation we endure from the rest of our species.

Friendship is a rare and fading phenomenon in a world of text messaging, Facebook relationships, and pseudo friendships. Possibly I still live in some idealistic fantasy about friendships that endure and where the rules of true brotherhood are respected, but I'm wired that way and I have to respect my own essence.

Fortunately, in spite of the seemingly endless disappointments that life provides, and the many great loves and friendships that have faded from all of our lives, there are some people who last. Their friendship endures, and they make all the disappointing relationships more tolerable. These special connections are critical to feeling a sense of comradeship on this planet.

These relationships happen without planning and create the basis for much of the good in our lives. Hopefully, some of these true friends can be our relatives but that is not always guaranteed. Acknowledging that it isn't always possible to have enduring bonds with our parents, siblings, or our children, leaves one to seek these intimate relationships elsewhere.

Possibly the bonds of friendship are one of the true joys that help us tolerate and cope with the losses and disappointments of the life cycle.

I have made it a practice to consider my patients to be friends in a special category. This allows the hours spent together to be more than just work. Although only a few of my patients ever become friends in the years following their treatment, this concept has made me feel a certain caring that I don't always see demonstrated in my fellow psychologists.

Either way, friends do shield us from the glare of life's harsher moments and make us feel a little less alone. So enjoy as many people as you can. It's good for your health.

ALL SUFFERING COMES FROM NOT ACCEPTING "WHAT IS"

I wish I could claim this statement as my own, but it is a Buddhist principle that has gained a certain degree of following among new age thinkers. In spite of its universal acceptance among Eastern philosophy advocates, I feel it is such a critical comment on the world process and so valuable in terms of the centering process this book espouses, that including it on my Laundry List would be forgivable.

There are certain universal facts that preclude argument. One is that we age daily and the end product of life is its end. Also that life circumstances involve adjusting to constant change. High school ends abruptly and we are thrown into a new reality of continuous challenges. Our relatives and friends who raised us die and we are left to cope with these losses.

Our children grow up and, with our blessings and hope, depart and create their own families. The telling signs of continuous change are evident when we sentimentally open the albums of our children's photos of their early days and years. Those of us who embrace change, learn to appreciate the current stage of our children's lives and smile when we recall their younger years.

The acceptance of the loss of loved ones and friends to death, led me to writing "The Eggs in Your Basket" in my last book, *Happiness A Positive Addiction*. It was an attempt to help patients cope with the excruciating acceptance that the human life of a young child had ended abruptly. There are other acceptances that are less definite than death but just as life defining.

The most common and classic is the emotionally wrenching experience of divorce. It is a life event that can be devastating until one accepts the ramifications of the divorce process. The suffering of a divorcee relates directly to the illusion, one commonly promoted in contemporary literature, that romantic love is eternal. This illusion leads to the statement during the marriage ceremony that we will be together "until death do us part".

The acceptance of divorce drags one through the stages of emotional turmoil one encounters with the death of a loved one. In the case of divorce, it is the death of an agreement frequently made based on passion and impulse which cannot stand the test of time.

Most of us have experienced the sense of betrayal which accompanies the loss of a love connection. The suffering that love creates is a lesson of basic Buddhism. It is described as a cycle of suffering the Buddha outlines in his general points for liberation. The attachment to people, things, and ideas ultimately always leads to some sense of loss and betrayal.

The Laundry List

Marriage, to many of us, was the idea of security, companionship, and love. The destruction of the idea of permanent love and its end can plunge a normal individual into despair, suicidal, and homicidal behavior, frequently accompanied by the abyss of self pity.

The ramification of break-ups, and the deception frequently accompanying them, keeps psychologist's offices busy and police stations active between domestic calls and the more tragic murders and suicides that, more than occasionally, accompany divorce and relationship break-ups.

So what can I offer, if anything, to young people entering the realm of life that concerns itself with committed relationships. These relationships need interpersonal work as well as the use of mentors, psychologists, or marriage counselors when necessary. Romantic relationships often don't last a lifetime and we need to stop blaming ourselves for the end of romantic love. Personally,. I have with time become capable of smiling about the impermanence of love based primarily upon passion and learned to enjoy the memories connected with these episodes that transpired during my earlier years.

The realization that lovers and friends will eventually fade from a focal point in our lives to almost complete oblivion, is an indication that one has experienced life fully. My happiness must be predicated on activities I do daily, not others. These activities involve my devotion to meditation, yoga, swimming, hiking, my family, and my patients. I strongly recommended that you plan for change and learn to embrace it by developing activities which you control directly.

Another, and most critical, inevitable change is aging and the continuing redefinition of role which accompanies the life cycle. We leave the nest, start our own families, our children grow and leave. As I commented earlier in this chapter, our friends age and depart, as we will, into the unknown world of death. What is, is that we are alive today and we have an ultimate responsibility to embrace each day as it is without expectation. Living this way will create the acceptance necessary to overcome suffering and to allow us to realize the universe has created a wonderful entity for us to live on – if we do so without expectation or desire.

The Laundry List

WHETHER YOUR LIFE MEANS ANYTHING IS COMPLETELY UP TO YOU

The impact of that idea struck me at the age of 10. I was walking alone back to the dormitories of Lake Grove School, a private boarding school in Smithtown Long Island. It was a cool autumn day and a sense of aloneness, which I had experienced a great deal of as a child, was thrust upon me. That aloneness seemed extremely poignant at that moment. Living away from the security of parents at an early age makes a child grow up rather quickly. The thought about my future that came to me that November day was that no one really cared what happened to me and whatever my life would be was completely up to me. Surprisingly, the thought did not make me feel sad. It opened the door to the somewhat premature introspection that my life was up to me and that, if I wanted to make something out of myself, I would have to be the catalyst of that process.

It was good, in retrospect, just to see life's realities early. This moment of existential clarity and self-confrontation proved to be a good elixir for self pity. I jokingly referred to my boarding school years as "foster care for the rich" but now I am sure that that autumn walk has helped me for many years in developing my identity.

The Laundry List

We are all ultimately responsible for our own life's purpose, or lack of. The sooner we confront that issue, the more likely we will come up with a reasonable answer to our personal dilemma.

The even more perplexing aspect of whether your life has any meaning or not is that the issue needs ongoing revision throughout the life cycle. There are different challenges presented at different periods of one's life. Early adulthood is based on establishing identity, choosing work, and finding a spouse. I do mean choosing work as so many people seem to allow themselves to just work a job they find meaningless and uninspiring.

Then there is the decision to create a family and the massive commitment of time and resources the raising of children requires. This may be your meaning for many years but ultimately the children grow up and the question of "what now?" becomes pressing. Each developmental stage of life demands confronting what your life means now.

Clearly, poverty makes surviving the paramount task for many but I have seen people who have created goals and, through their will and desire, rose above their impoverished childhoods. They saw possibilities and strove for something more while their peers were willing to accept the status quo. What created the desire for these people to push themselves is rather mysterious. It is as if they had an inner dreamer that the person listened to that another seemed to ignore.

The Laundry List

It is too easy for me to say the goal of life is getting to Heaven, God, or Nirvana. I have no idea whether any of these actually exist in fact, and neither do you, although you may hope they do. It is better to work with what is, establish what you want from this life, set goals and achieve them. If there is a bonus afterlife, that's fine, but the reason you are here now is up to you so you must grapple with that, find your unique gifts, and fully explore your potentials while you still can.

The Laundry List

IF YOU REALLY WANTED IT, YOU WOULD ALREADY HAVE IT

Once again we are addressing the issue of self-confrontation and self honesty. I have sat listening to literally thousands of my fellow humans who have confessed that somehow their lives haven't turned out the way they wanted. The things they claim they wanted out of life were somehow unachievable in spite of their efforts to acquire them.

This is particularly true with people who can't seem to find the "right person" to make a life commitment to. These souls sadly share their stories of disappointing relationships and unfulfilled promises. As the years go by, many of the love-deprived give up trying or just keep repeating, over and over again, the same unsuccessful patterns that have led to where they are. It is almost like using a key that doesn't fit to open a door and refusing to acknowledge the futility of your efforts.

Similarly, if you really want more money, a new career, a different life, you could pay the price to acquire it. Sometimes massive amounts of effort may be called upon but if you really wanted it enough, the effort would be made. The truth in most cases is that the idea is appealing but we are unwilling to pay the price.

The Laundry List

In watching people frantically seeking each other, the idea of carefully observing one's approach is critical and seldom do individuals face the consequences of the way they approach relationships. If we want to find the right person, we would work on ourselves, our approach, our neediness, and our desperation.

Two particular women I am currently treating come to mind. No matter how often we review the self-defeating patterns of their relationship choices, they seem deeply committed to not changing their behavior. Their conduct literally sabotages any hope of their achieving the security and companionship they claim they want. Ultimately, after each failure, they return to more self-criticism and self-debasement in front of me; another key component in not achieving their goals.

So be in good faith, meaning self honesty, concerning the things you claim you want. Were they important enough for you to commit yourself to achieve them? Failure means more effort. Success is ultimately a product of self-satisfaction, a concept very foreign to the materialism we were all raised in.

The life you have can be different if you want it to be but that takes great effort. Are you willing to make the effort? Please think for a moment before you reply.

The Laundry List

LEARNING TO STOP JUDGING LEAVES LOTS OF ROOM TO LEARN

We all have our inner judge. The judge becomes part of our personality so early in our lives that we never have a chance to have any input into its formation and prejudices.

There are many terms in psychology to describe the inner judge. Freud called it "the super ego", Fritz Perls in Gestalt Therapy described the judge as "top dog". Eric Berne in his Transactional Analysis format described the judge as "the critical parent in all of us".

No matter what label we put on the judge, it divides the world into dualities, good-bad, ugly-beautiful, and endless other ways we separate ourselves and define the walls from which we disconnect from others and the world around us. It is remarkable how, in my psychologist/counselor role, I can adamantly attempt to eliminate the judge, but when I am asked to determine a person's disability or psychiatric diagnosis, the judge leaps to the forefront again. It is almost as if my judge is a hat I can choose to wear or take off at my option.

The realization that being in my judgmental self, or not, was up to me, was quite liberating. The fact that we can stop the judge from literally ruling our consciousness is one of the first steps toward opening ourselves up to the possibility of expansion and learning. The basic contents of the judge's prejudices are racial and cultural as well as attitudes about attractiveness and what appeals to us or not.

The judge endlessly determines our way of looking at the world around us and creates our own inner reality. The Eastern mind, promoted by the works of Buddhists and Taoists, discusses the possibility of non-dual reality. Seeing things without judging, observing without labels, creates the possibility of relearning our reactions to the world around us.

The value of opening ourselves up to the world has remarkable benefits. It offers the possibility of our becoming more than what we were programmed to be by our parents, schools, and our ethnic background.

Unfortunately the judge, just like other parts of our inner psyche, is a lifetime companion. We can work on reforming our judge but he will pop up at the most inconvenient moments and can hurt others and separate us from connecting to the world around us.

Fortunately, learning to observe our stream of consciousness through meditation and self-observational work makes understanding the judge possible. This introspectional learning ultimately helps in making us stop taking the judge's pronouncements so seriously. Once we began to laugh at the

The Laundry List

judge, we begin to realize that many of our own inner prejudices, in terms of the big picture of the universe, have very little meaning whatsoever.

The Laundry List

The Laundry List

HAPPY PEOPLE HAVE ACQUIRED THE RIGHT WAY TO THINK, LIVE, AND FEEL

Living in a joyful manner is not an accident. People acquire attitudes and behaviors that foster joyful moments and I'd like to share some of the ways that I have witnessed to facilitate this process.

There are some basic principles that hopefully you have extracted from the Laundry List. Before I end our journey together, I'd like to summarize them and then share what I have seen in my work that seems to work to make life richer and more complete.

One's commitment to enjoy the day, every day, leads to learning to find moments and activities to appreciate being. Those artistically talented achieve this through their creative processes. However, not all of us are gifted in this manner so we don't have that spark of magic in painting, sculpting, writing, creating or playing music. I have, however, seen that sense of accomplishment in a carpenter looking at his finished product, or the joy of a student who has completed a term paper at the end of a semester. There are endless ways humans can achieve a sense of mastery. You don't have to be Beethoven or Picasso to enjoy a creative act.

The Laundry List

Another key ingredient seems to be the appreciation of the simple act of living on the planet on a daily basis. Recent research at the University of North Carolina reached the conclusion that happy people do not need to be Pollyanna or deny the upsetting parts of life, but these people have the ability to put greater stock into small, happy moments daily. Savoring little pleasurable events in everyday life protects them from life's inevitable disappointments.

Loving others, not always the easiest human act but clearly a core component of a full life, is an essential part of the journey to an enriched, happy existence. Not just romantic love, as that creates inevitable highs and lows, but caring in a devoted way about other humans – be they your children, friends, relatives and, in my case, patients. It opens up a loving soul connection between us which creates a sense of purpose.

This caring extends to animals, nature, and our environment; loving the joys of a nature hike and its subtle rewards, or the music of the birds each morning when we arise, searching for a heartfelt connection with the world and avoiding places, people and situations that inhibit the loving process from occurring.

Another key element in the Laundry List is letting the past go and moving on by taking responsibility for the reality that you are ultimately capable of molding your life in the here and now, without using the endless events of the past as justification for your unhappiness.

The Laundry List

Working on acquiring the right way to think, live, and feel, makes us more grateful and enthusiastic about our daily existence. It's not that happy people are markedly different from others but they are far more grateful to be on the planet and show active enthusiastic lives which buffer them from the suffering which is inevitable. They accept the full spectrum of life's possibilities and wake up looking forward to another day – whether it be a vacation, work or weekend day. They all count the same.

There are so many little things that make being here worthwhile. We just have to pay attention. I recall the James Taylor song with the words, "The secret of life is enjoying the passing of time". This may seem incredibly simple but its simplicity is why it is so important.

Hopefully, my readers will discover some creature in nature which will also do that for you.

The Laundry List

The Laundry List

Here are other fine books written by Kenneth Garett, Ph.D.

Happiness A Positive Addiction
A guide to understanding what it takes to be truly happy.

Relationship Styles and Patterns
Kenneth Garett, Ph.D. and William Rose, Ph.D.
Explore the fascinating patterns of your unique Relationship Styles with Drs. Garett and Rose.

You Are Already Perfect!
Kenneth Garett, Ph.D. In this book Dr. Garret, writes how and why, You Are Already Perfect. Ken shares insights and logic culminated by Zen Masters to help, ease and ultimately comfort.

Julio and Schwartz, A Brooklyn Friendship
Kenneth Garett, Ph.D.
Ken writes a fun and humorous novel that explores the meaning and importance of friendships.

For more information regarding any of these books or to contact the author call: (760) 327-9566, or visit our website at:
www.Wmpbooks.com

Williams Publishing
31822 Village Center Road, Suite 102
Westlake Village, California 91361
(818) 889-8800

About Dr. Garett...

Kenneth Garett, Ph.D. is a psychologist, lecturer, and author. He has written four books and numerous articles concerning personal growth, self improvement, and relationships.

Dr. Garett was born in New York City. He attended Boston University for his undergraduate degree, received his Master's Degree from the University of the Americas in Mexico, finally completing his Doctoral Degree at the University of Southern California at Los Angeles.

He traveled to India, as a young man, and studied Yoga with B.K.S. Iyengar in Poona, India.

For the past 35 years, Dr. Garett has been a researcher and understands the dynamics of substance abuse in families. He has been a consulting neuropsychologist and clinical evaluator at the Betty Ford Center in Rancho Mirage, California. He has lectured and taught at universities, governmental agencies, and for airlines and other corporate sponsors both nationally and abroad.

He is a thought-provoking scholar whose books have been considered important practical guides for those seeking direction and creating a dynamic and purposeful existence.

Dr. Garett, and his colleagues, maintain a multidisciplinary mental health setting in Palm Springs, California. His emphasis is positive life skills acquisition and life satisfaction development training.

www.ingramcontent.com/pod-product-compliance
Lightning Source LLC
Chambersburg PA
CBHW071831290426
44109CB00017B/1793